Chronicle

The Historie of England (1 o ... ... une Time That It Was First Inhabited, Vntill the Time That It Was Last Conquered: Wherein the Sundrie Alterations of the State Vnder Forren People Is Declared; And Other Manifold Observations Remembred

Raphael Holinshed

Alpha Editions

This edition published in 2024

ISBN : 9789367244616

Design and Setting By
Alpha Editions
www.alphaedis.com
Email - info@alphaedis.com

Contents

THE FIRST CHAPTER.

What manner of people did first inhabite this our country, which hath most generallie and of longest continuance béene knowne among all nations by the name of Britaine as yet is not certeinly knowne; neither can it be decided frō whence the first inhabitants there of came, by reason of such diuersitie in iudgements as haue risen amongst the learned in this The originall of nations for the most part vncerteine. behalfe. But sith the originall in maner of all nations is doubtfull, and euen the same for the more part fabulous (that alwaies excepted which we find in the holie scriptures) I wish not any man to leane to that which shall be here set downe as to an infallible truth, sith I doo but onlie shew other mens conjectures, grounded neuerthelesse vpon likelie reasons, concerning that matter whereof there is now left but little other certeintie, or rather none at all.

Whither Britaine were an Iland at the first. *Geog. com. lib.* No Ilands at the first, as some coniecture. To fetch therefore the matter from the farthest, and so to stretch it forward, it séemeth by the report of Dominicus Marius Niger that in the beginning, when God framed the world, and diuided the waters apart from the earth, this Ile was then a parcell of the continent, and ioined without any separation of sea to the maine land. But this opinion (as all other the like vncerteinties) I leaue to be discussed of by the learned: howbeit for the first inhabitation of this Ile with people, I haue thought good to set downe in part, what may be gathered out of such writers as haue touched that matter, and may séeme to giue some light vnto the knowledge thereof.

In the first part of the acts of the English votaries. Britaine inhabitied before the floud. *Genesis 6. Berosus ant. lib.* 1. First therefore Iohn Bale our countrieman, who in his time greatlie trauelled in the search of such antiquities, dooth probablie coniecture, that this land was inhabited and replenished with people long before the floud, at that time in the which the generation of mankind (as Moses writeth) began to multiplie vpon the vniuersall face of the earth: and therfore it followeth, that as well this land was inhabited with people long before the daies of Noah, as any the other countries and parts of the world beside. But when they had once forsaken the ordinances appointed them by God, and betaken them to new waies inuented of themselues, such loosenesse of life ensued euerie where, as brought vpon them the great deluge and vniuersall floud, in the which perished as well the inhabitants of these quarters, as the residue of the race of mankind, generallie dispersed in euerie other part of the whole world, onelie Noah & his familie excepted, who by the prouidence and pleasure of almightie God was preserued from the rage of those waters, to recontinue and repaire the new generation of man of vpon earth.

Noah. *In comment. super 4. lib. Berosus de antiquit. lib. 1 Annius vt suor.* After the flood (as Annius de Viterbo recordeth) and reason also enforceth, Noah was the onlie monarch of all the world, and as the same Annius gathereth by the account of Moses in the 100. yeare after the flood, Noah diuided the earth among his thrée sonnes; assigning to the possession of his eldest sonne all that portion of land which now is knowne by the name of Asia; to his second sonne Cham, he appointed all that part of the world which now is called Affrica: and to his third sonne Iaphet was allotted all Europa, with all the Iles therto belonging, wherin among other was conteined this our Ile of Britaine, with the other Iles thereto perteining.

IAPHET AND HIS SONNES. *Johannes Bodinus ad fac. hist. cogn. Franciscus Tarapha.* Iaphet the third son of Noah, of some called Iapetus, and of others, Atlas Maurus (because he departed this life in Mauritania) was the first (as Bodinus affirmeth by the authoritie and consent of the Hebrue, Gréeke & Latine writers) that peopled the countries of Europe, which afterward he diuided among his sonnes: of whom Tuball (as Tarapha affirmeth) obteined the kingdome of Spaine. Gomer had dominion ouer the Italians, and (as Berosus and diuers other authors agrée) Samothes was the founder of Celtica, which conteined in it (as Bale witnesseth) a great part of Europe, but speciallie those countries which now are called by the names of Gallia and Britannia.

Britaine inhabited shortlie after the floud. Thus was this Iland inhabited and peopled within 200 yéeres after the floud by the children of Iaphet the sonne of Noah: & this is not onlie prooued by Annius, writing vpon Berosus, but also confirmed by Moses in the scripture, where he writeth, that of the offspring of Iaphet, the Iles of the Gentiles (wherof Britain is one) were sorted into regions in the time of Phaleg the sonne of Hiber, who was borne at the time of the *Theophilus episcop. Antioch. ad Anfol lib. 2.* The words of Theophilus a doctor of the church, who liued an. Dom. 160. diuision of languages. Herevpon Theophilus hath these words: "Cùm priscis temporibus pauci forent homines in Arabia & Chaldæa, post linguarum diuisionem aucti & multiplicati paulatim sunt: hinc quidam abierunt versus orientem, quidam concessere ad partes maioris continentis, alij porrò profecti sunt ad septentrionem sedes quæsituri, nec priùs desierunt terram vbiq; occupare, quàm etiam Britannos in Arctois climatibus accesserint, &c." *That is;* "When at the first there were not manie men in Arabia and Chaldæa, it came to passe, that after the diuision of toongs, they began somewhat better to increase and multiplie, by which occasion some of them went toward the east, and some toward the parts of the great maine land: diuers of them went also northwards to seeke them dwelling places, neither staid they to replenish the earth as they went, till they came vnto the Iles of Britaine, lieng vnder the north pole." Thus far Theophilus.

These things considered, Gildas the Britaine had great reason to thinke, that this countrie had bene inhabited from the beginning. And Polydor Virgil was with no lesse consideration hereby induced to confesse, that the Ile of Britaine had receiued inhabitants foorthwith after the floud.

Of Samothes, Magus, Sarron, Druis, and Bardus, fiue kings succeeding each other in regiment ouer the Celts and Samotheans, and how manie hundred yeeres the Celts inhabited this Iland.

THE SECOND CHAPTER.

Gen. 2. Samothes the sixt begotten sonne of Iaphet called by Moses Mesech, by *De migr. gen.* others Dis, receiued for his portion (according to the report of Wolfgangus Lazius) all the countrie lieng betwéene the riuer of Rhene and the Pyrenian mountains, where he founded the kingdome of Celtica *Cent. 1.* ouer his people called Celtæ. Which name Bale affirmeth to haue bene indifferent to the inhabitants both of the countrie of Gallia, and the *Anti. lib. 1. Bale Script. Brit. cent.1.* Ile of Britaine, & that he planted colonies of men (brought foorth of the east parts) in either of them, first in the maine land, and after in the Iland. He is reported by Berosus to haue excelled all men of that age in learning and knowledge: and also is thought by Bale to haue imparted the same among his people; namelie, the vnderstanding *Cæsar. comment. lib.8.* of the sundrie courses of the starres, the order of inferiour things, with manie other matters incident to the morall and politike gouernment of mans life: and to haue deliuered the same in the Phenician letters: out of which the Gréekes (according to the opinion of Archilochus) *In epithet. temp. De æquinorus contra Appionem.* deuised & deriued the Gréeke characters, insomuch that Xenophon and Iosephus doo constantlie report (although Diogenes Laertius be against it) that both the Gréekes and other nations receiued their letters and learning first from these countries. Of this king and his learning arose *Lib. de Magic. success. lib. 22.* a sect of philosophers (saith Annius) first in Britaine, and after in Gallia, the which of his name were called Samothei. They (as Aristotle and Secion write) were passing skilfull both in the law of God and man: *Script. Brit. cent. I.* and for that cause excéedinglie giuen to religion, especiallie the inhabitants of this Ile of Britaine, insomuch that the whole nation did not onelie take the name of them, but the Iland it selfe (as Bale *De ant. Cant. cent. lib. I.* and doctor Caius agree) came to be called Samothea, which was the first peculiar name that euer it had, and by the which it was especiallie *This Ile called Samothea.* knowne before the arriuall of Albion.

MAGUS THE SON OF SAMOTHES. *Lib. 9. Annius in commen. super eundem. Geogr.* Magus the sonne of Samothes, after the death of his father, was the second king of Celtica, by whome (as Berosus writeth) there were manie townes builded among the Celts, which by the witnesse of Annius did beare the addition of their founder Magus: of which townes diuers are to be found in Ptolomie. And Antoninus a painfull surueior of the world and searcher of cities, maketh mention of foure of them here in Britaine, Sitomagus, Neomagus, Niomagus, and Nouiomagus. Neomagus sir Thomas Eliot writeth to haue stood where the citie of Chester now standeth; Niomagus, George Lillie placeth where the towne of Buckingham is now remaining. Beside this, Bale dooth so highlie commend the foresaid Magus for his learning renowmed ouer all the world, that he would haue the Persians, and other nations of the south and west parts, to deriue the name of their diuines called *Magi* from him. In déed Rauisius Textor, and sir Iohn Prise affirme, that in the daies of Plinie, the Britons were so expert in art magike, that they might be thought to haue first deliuered the same to the Persians. What the name of *Magus De diui. lib. 1. De fastis li. 5.* importeth, and of what profession the *Magi* were, Tullie declareth at large, and Mantuan in briefe, after this maner:

Ille penes Persas Magus est, qui sidera norit,
Qui sciat herbarum vires cultúmq; deorum,
Persepoli facit ista Magos prudentia triplex.

The Persians terme him Magus, that
the course of starres dooth knowe,
The power of herbs, and worship due
   to God that man dooth owe,
By threefold knowledge thus the name
   of Magus then dooth growe. *H.F.*

SARRON THE SON OF MAGUS. *De ant. Cant. lib. 1.* Bale. script. Brit. cent. I. Sarron the third king of the Celts succéeded his father Magus in gouernement of the countrie of Gallia, and the Ile Samothea, wherein as (D. Caius writeth) he founded certaine publike places for them that professed learning, which Berosus affirmeth to be done, to the intent to restraine the wilfull outrage of men, being as then but raw and void of all ciuilitie. Also it is thought by Annius, that he was the first author of those kind of philosophers, which were called Sarronides, of whom Diodorus Siculus writeth in this sort: "There are (saith he) among Lib. 6. the Celts certaine diuines and philosophers called Sarronides, whom aboue all other they haue in great estimation. For it is the manner among them, not without a philosopher to make anie sacrifice: sith they are of beléefe, that sacrifices ought onelie to be made by such as are skilfull in the diuine mysteries, as of those who are néerest vnto God, by whose intercession they thinke all good things are to be required of God, and whose aduise they vse and follow, as well in warre as in peace."

DRUIS THE SON OF SARRON. *De morte Claud.* Druis, whom Seneca calleth Dryus, being the sonne of Sarron, was after his father established the fourth king of Celtica, indifferentlie reigning as wel ouer the Celts as Britons, or rather (as the inhabitants of this Ile were then called) Samotheans. This prince is commended by Berosus to be so plentifullie indued with wisedome and learning, that Annius taketh him to be the vndoubted author of the begining and name of the philosophers called Druides, whome Cæsar and all other ancient Gréeke and Latine writers doo affirme to haue had their begining in Britaine, and to haue bin brought from thence into Gallia, insomuch that when there arose any doubt in that countrie touching any point of their discipline, they did repaire to be resolued therein into Britaine, where, speciallie in the Ile of Anglesey (as Humfrey Llhoyd witnesseth) they *Anti. lib. 5. Annius super eundem. De bello Gallico. lib. 9. De bello Gallico. 6.* made their principall abode. Touching their vsages many things are written by Aristotle, Socion, Plinie, Laertius, Bodinus, and others: which I will gather in briefe, and set downe as followeth. They had (as Cæsar saith) the charge of common & priuate sacrifices, the discussing of points of religion, the bringing vp of youth, the determining of matters in variance with full power to interdict so manie from the sacrifice of their gods and the companie of men, as disobeied *Hist. an. lib. 1.* their award. Polydore affirmeth, how they taught, that mens soules could not die, but departed from one bodie to another, and that to the intent *De diui. lib. 1.* to make men valiant and dreadlesse of death. Tullie writeth, that partlie by tokens, and partlie by surmises, they would foretell things to come. And by the report of Hector Boetius, some of them were not ignorant of the immortalitie of the one and euerlasting God. All these *Hist. Scoti. li. 2. De migr. gen. lib. 2. Marcellinus.* things they had written in the Greeke toong, insomuch that Wolf. Lazius (vpon the report of Marcellinus) declareth how the Gréeke letters were first brought to Athens by Timagenes from the Druides. And herevpon it commeth also to passe, that the British toong hath in it remaining at this day some smacke of the Gréeke. Among other abuses of the Druides, they had (according to Diodorus) one custome to kill men, and by the falling, bleeding, and dismembring of them, to diuine of things to come: for the which and other wicked practises, their sect was first condemned for abhominable (as some haue written) and dissolued in Gallia (as Auentinus witnesseth) by Tiberius and Claudius the emperours; and *Anna. Boiorum. lib. 22.* lastlie abolished here in Britaine (by the report of Caius) when the gospell of Christ by the preaching of Fugatius and Damianus was receiued *De ant. Cant.* among the Britaines, vnder Lucius king of Britaine, about the yeare of our sauior, 179.

BARDUS THE SONNE OF DRUIS. *Berosus ant. lib. 2. Annius in commen. super eundem. Ant. Cant li. 1. script. Britan. cent. 1. Nonnius. Marcel. Strabo. Diodor. Sicul. lib. 6. Carol. Stepha. in dict. hist. Bale. Iohn Prise.* Bardus the sonne of Druis succéeded his father in the kingdome of Celtica, and was the fift king ouer the Celtes and Samotheans, amongst whom he was highlie renoumed (as appeareth by Berosus) for inuention of dities and musicke, wherein Annius of Viterbo writeth, that he trained his people: and of such as excelled in this knowledge, he made an order of philosophicall poets or heraulds, calling them by his owne name Bardi. And it should séeme by doctor Caius and master Bale, that Cæsar found some of them here at his arriuall in this Ile, and reported that they had also their first begining in the same. The profession and vsages of these Bardi, Nonnius, Strabo, Diodorus, Stephanus,

Bale, and sir Iohn Prise, are in effect reported after this sort. They did vse to record the noble exploits of the ancient capteins, and to drawe the pedegrées and genealogies of such as were liuing. They would frame pleasant dities and songs, learne the same by heart, and sing them to instruments at solemne feasts and assemblies of noble men and gentlemen. Wherefore they were had in so high estimation, that if two hosts had bene readie ranged to ioine in battell, and that any of them had fortuned to enter among them, both the hosts (as well the enimies as the friends) would haue holden their hands, giuen eare vnto them, and ceassed from fight, vntill these Bards *Lucan. lib. 1.* had gone out of the battell. Of these Bards Lucane saith,

Vos quoq; qui fortes animas bellóq; peremptas,
Laudius in longum vares dimittítis æuum,
Plurima securi fudistis carmina Bardi:

II. F. And you ô poet Bards from danger
   void that dities sound,
Of soules of dreadlesse men, whom rage
   of battell would confound,
And make their lasting praise to time
   of later age rebound.

Because the names of these poets were neither discrepant from the ciuilitie of the Romans, nor repugnant to the religion of the Christians, they (of all the other sects before specified) were suffered onlie to continue vnabolished in all ages, insomuch that there flourished of them among the Britains (according to Bale) before the birth of Christ, *Iohn Bale script. Britan. cent. 2. John Prise defen hist. Brit. Caius de ant. Cant. lib. 1. Iohn Leland syllab. ant dict. Hum. Lloyd de Mona insula* Plenidius and Oronius: after Christ (as Prise recounteth) Thalestine, and the two Merlins, Melkin, Elaskirion, and others: and of late daies among the Welshmen, Dauid Die, Ioslo Gough, Dauid ap William, with an infinite number more. And in Wales there are sundrie of them (as Caius reporteth) remaining vnto this day, where they are in their language called (as Leland writeth) Barthes. Also by the witnes of Humfrey Llhoyd, there is an Iland néere vnto Wales, called Insula Bardorum, and Bardsey, whereof the one name in Latine, and the other in Saxon or old English, signifieth the Iland of the Bardes or Barthes.

Thus farré the gouernement of the Celts in this Ile

AN APPENDIX TO THE FORMER CHAPTER.

Bale After Bardus, the Celts (as Bale saith) loathing the streict ordinances of their ancient kings, and betaking themselues to pleasure and idlenesse, were in short time, and with small labour brought vnder the subiection of the giant Albion, the sonne of Neptune, who altering the state of things in this Iland, streicted the name of Celtica and the Celts within the bounds of Gallia, from whence they came first to inhabit this land vnder the conduct of Samothes, as before ye haue heard, accordinglie as Annius *Annius* hath gathered out of Berosus the Chaldean, who therein agréeth also with *Theophilus.* the scripture, the saieng of Theophilus the doctor, and the generall consent of all writers, which fullie consent, that the first inhabitants of this Ile came out of the parties of Gallia, although some of them dissent about the time and maner of their comming. Sir Brian Tuke *Sir Brian Tuke* thinketh it to be ment of the arriuall   of   Brute,   when   he   came   out   of   *Cæsar.* those countries into this Ile. Cæsar and Tacitus seeme to be of opinion, that those Celts which first inhabited here, came ouer to view the *Tacitus. Bodinus.* countrie for trade of merchandize. Bodinus would haue them to come in (a Gods name) from Languedoc, and so to name this land Albion, of a citie in *Beda. Polydor.* Languedoc named Albie. Beda, and likewise Polydore (who followeth him) affirme that they came from the coasts of Armorica, which is now called little Britaine.

But that the authorities afore recited are sufficient to proue the time that this Iland was first inhabited by the Celts, the old possessors of Gallia; not onelie the néernesse of the regions, but the congruence of languages, two great arguments of originals doo fullie confirme *Bodinus.* the same. Bodinus writeth vpon report, that the British and Celtike language was all one. But whether that be true or not, I am not able to affirme, bicause the Celtike toong is long sithens growne wholie out of vse. Howbeit some such Celtike words as remaine in the writings of old authours may be perceiued to agrée with the Welsh toong, being the *Pausanias* vncorrupted spéech of the ancient Britains. In déed Pausanias the Grecian maketh mention how the Celts in their language called a horsse *Marc:* and by that name doo the Welshmen call a horsse to this day: and the word *Trimarc* in Pausanias, signifieth in the Celtike toong, thrée horsses.

Thus it appeared by the authoritie of writers, by situation of place, and by affinitie of language, that this Iland was first found and inhabited by the Celts, that there name from Samothes to Albion continued here the space of 310 yeares or there abouts. And finallie it is likelie, *Iohn Bale.* that aswell the progenie as the spéech of them is partlie remaining in this Ile among the inhabitants, and speciallie the British, euen vnto this day.

Of the giant Albion, of his comming into this Iland, diuers opinions why it was called Albion: why Albion and Bergion were slaine by Hercules: of Danaus and of his 50 daughters.

THE THIRD CHAPTER.

Bale. Annius de Viterbo. Diodorus Sicubis. Pinnesses or gallies. *Higinus. Pictonius.* Neptunus called by Moses (as some take it) Nepthuim, the sixt sonne of Osiris, after the account of Annius, and the brother of Hercules, had appointed him of his father (as Diodorus writeth) the gouernement of the ocean sea: wherefore he furnished himselfe of sundrie light ships for the more redie passage by water, which in the end grew to the number of a full nauie: & so by continuall exercise he became so skilfull, and therewith so mightie vpon the waters (as Higinus & Pictonius doo write) that he was not onelie called the king, but also estéemed the god of the seas. He had to wife a ladie called Amphitrita, who was also honored as goddesse of the seas, of whose bodie he begat sundrie children: and (as Bale reporteth) he made euerie *Scrip. Bri. cent.* 1. one of them king of an Iland. In the Ile of Britaine he landed his fourth son called Albion the giant, who brought the same vnder his subjection. *Ioh. Textor. Polydor.* And herevpon it resteth, that Iohn Textor, and Polydor Virgil made mention, that light shippes were first inuented in the British seas, and that the same were couered round with the hides of beasts, for defending them from the surges and waues of the water.

This Albion being put by his father in possession of this Ile of Britaine, within short time subdued the Samotheans, the first inhabitantes thereof, without finding any great resistance, for that (as before ye haue heard) they had giuen ouer the practise of all warlike and other painefull exercises, and through vse of effeminate pleasures, wherevnto they had giuen themselues ouer, they were become now vnapt to withstand the force of their enimies: and so (by the testimonie of *Nichol. Perot. Rigmanus Philesius. Aristotle. Hum Lhoyd.* Nicholaus Perottus, Rigmanus Philesius, Aristotle, and Humfrey Llhoyd, with diuers other, both forraine & home-writers) this Iland was first called by the name of Albion, hauing at one time both the name and inhabitants changed from the line of Iaphet vnto the accursed race of Cham.

This Albion (that thus changed the name of this Ile) and his companie, are called giants, which signifieth none other than a tall kind of men, of that vncorrupt stature and highnesse naturallie incident to the first *Berosus.* age (which Berosus also séemeth to allow, where he writeth, that Noah was one of the giants) and were not so called only of their monstrous greatnesse, as the common people thinke (although in deed they exceeded the vsuall stature of men now in these daies) but also for that they tooke their name of the soile where they were borne: for *Gigantes* What *Gigantes* signifie signifieth the sons of the earth: the Aborigines, or (as Cesar calleth them) Indigenæ; that is, borne and bred out of the earth where they inhabited.

Thus some thinke, but verelie although that their opinion is not to be allowed in any condition, which maintaine that there should be any *Against the opinion of the Aborigines.* Aborigines, or other kind of men than those of Adams line; yet that there haue béene men of far greater stature than are now to be found, is sufficientlie prooued by the huge bones of those that haue beene found in our time, or lately before: whereof here to make further relation it shall not need, sith in the description of Britaine ye shall find it sufficientlie declared. *Bale.* Bergion brother to Albion. Hercules Lybicus. But now to our purpose. As Albion held Britaine in subiecteith, so his brother Bergion kept Ireland and the Orkenies vnder his rule and dominion, and hearing that their coosine Hercules Lybicus hauing finished his conquests in Spaine, meant to passe through Gallia into Italie, against their brother Lestrigo that oppressed Italie, vnder subiection of him & other of his brethren the sons also of Neptune; as well Albion as Bergion assembling their powers togither, passed ouer into Gallia, to stoppe the passage of Hercules, whose intention was to vanquish and destroie those tyrants the sonnes of Neptune, & their complices that kept diuers countries and regions vnder the painefull yoke of their heauie thraldome.

The cause why Hercules pursued his cousins The cause that moued Hercules thus to pursue vpon those tyrants now reigning thus in the world, was, for that not long before, the greatest part of them had conspired togither and slaine his father Osiris, notwithstanding that they were nephues to the same Osiris, as sonnes to his brother Neptune, and not contented with his slaughter, they diuided his carcase also amongst them, so that each of them got a péece in token of reioising at their murtherous atchiued enterprise.

For this cause Hercules (whome Moses calleth Laabin) proclamed warres against them all in reuenge of his fathers death: and first he killed Triphon and Busiris in Aegypt, then Anteus in Mauritania, & the Gerions in Spaine, which enterprise atchined, he led his armie towardes Italie, and by the way passed through a part of Gallia, where Albion and Bergion *Pomp. Mela.* hauing vnited their powers togither, were readie to receiue him with battell: and so néere to the mouth of the riuer called Rhosne, in Latine *Rhodanus,* they met & fought. At the first there was a right terrible and cruell conflict betwixt them. And albeit that Hercules had the greatest number of men, yet was it verie doubtfull a great while, to whether part the glorie of that daies worke would bend. Whereupon when the victorie began outright to turne vnto Albion, and to his brother Bergion, Hercules perceiuing the danger and likelihood of vtter losse of that battell, speciallie for that his men had wasted their weapons, he caused those that stood still and were not otherwise occupied, to stoope downe, and to gather vp stones, whereof in that place there was great plentie, which by his commandement they bestowed so fréelie vpon Hercules discomfiteith his enimies. Albion is slaine their enimies, that in the end hée obteined the victorie, and did not only put his adversaries to flight, but also slue Albion there in the field, togither with his brother Bergion, and the most part of all their whole armie. This was the end of Albion, and his brother Bergion, by the valiant prowesse of Hercules, who as one appointed by Gods prouidence to subdue the cruell & vnmercifull tyrants, spent his time to the benefit of mankind, deliuering the oppressed from the heauie yoke of miserable thraldome, in euerie place where he came.

The occasion of the fable of Jupiter helping his son Hercules. And by the order of this battell wée maye learne whereof the poets had their inuention, when they faine in their writings, that Jupiter holpe his sonne Hercules, by throwing downe stones from heauen in this battell against Albion and Bergion. Moreouer, from henceforth was this Ile of How this Ile was called Albion, of the giant Albion. *Iohn Bale.* Britaine called Albion (as before we haue said) after the name of the said Albion: because he was established chiefe ruler and king thereof both by his grandfather Osiris and his father Neptune that cunning sailour reigning therein (as Bale saith) by the space of 44. yeares, till finally he was slaine in maner afore remembred by his vncle Hercules Libicus.

After that Hercules had thus vanquished and destroied his enimies, hée passed to and fro thorough Gallia, suppressing the tyrants in euerie part where he came, and restoring the people vnto a reasonable kinde of libertie, vnder lawfull gouernours. This Hercules (as we find) builded the citie Alexia in Burgongne, nowe called Alize. Moreouer, by Lilius Giraldus in the life of Hercules it is auouched, that the same Hercules came ouer hither into Britaine. And this dooth Giraldus write by warrant of such Britons as (saith he) haue so written themselues, which thing peraduenture he hath read in Gildas the ancient Briton poet: a booke that (as he confesseth in the 5. dialog of his histories of poets) he hath séene. The same thing also is confirmed by the name of an head of land in Britaine called *Promontorium Herculis,* as in Ptolomie ye may read, which is thought to take name of his arriuall at that place. Thus much for Albion and Hercules.

Diuers opinions why this Ile was called Albion. Sée more hereof in the discription. But now, whereas it is not denied of anie, that this Ile was called ancientlie by the name of Albion: yet there be diuers opinions how it came by that name: for manie doo not allow of this historie of Albion the giant. But for so much as it apperteineth rather to the description than to the historie of this Ile, to rip vp and lay foorth the secret mysteries of such matters: and because I thinke that this opinion which is here auouched, how it tooke that name of the forsaid Albion, sonne to Neptune, may be confirmed with as good authoritie as some of the other, I here passe ouer the rest, & procéed with the historie.

When Albion chiefe capteine of the giants was slaine, the residue that remained at home in the Ile, continued without any rule or restraint of law, in so much that they fell to such a dissolute order of life, that they séemed little or nothing to differ from brute beasts: and those are they which our ancient chronicles call the giants, who were so named, as well for the huge proportion of their stature (sithens as before is said, that age brought foorth far greater men than are now liuing) as also for that they were the first, or at the least the furthest in remembrance of any that had inhabited this countrie. For this word *Gigines,* or *Gegines,* from whence our word giant (as some take it) is deriued, is a Gréeke word, and signifieth, Borne or bred of or in the earth, for our fore-elders, specially the Gentiles, being ignorant of the true beginning of mankind, were persuaded, that the first inhabitants of any countrie were bred out of the earth, and therefore when they could go no higher, *Terræ filius* what it signifieth. reckoning the descents of their predecessours, they would name him *Terræ filius,* The sonne of the earth: and so the giants whom the poets faine to haue sought to make battell against heauen, are called the sonnes of the earth: and the first inhabitants generally of euery countrie were of the Gréekes called *Gigines,* or *Gegines,* and of the Latines *Aborigines. Indigenæ. Aborigines,* and *Indigenæ,* that is, People borne of the earth from the beginning, and comming from no other countrie, but bred within the same.

These giants and first inhabitants of this Ile continued in their beastlie kind of life vnto the arriuall of the ladies, which some of our chronicles ignorantly write to be the daughters of Dioclesian the king of Assyria, whereas in déed they haue béene deceiued, in taking the The mistaking of the name of Dioclesianus for Danaus. word *Danaus* to be short written for *Dioclesianus:* and by the same meanes haue diuers words and names béene mistaken, both in our chronicles, and in diuers other ancient written woorks. But this is a fault that learned men should not so much trouble themselues about, considering the *Hugh the Italian. Harding. Iohn Rous* out of *Dauid Pencair.* same hath bin alreadie found by sundrie authors ling sithens, as Hugh the Italian, Iohn Harding, Iohn Rouse of Warwike, and others, speciallie by the helpe of Dauid Pencair a British historie, who recite the historie vnder the name of Danaus and his daughters. And because we would not any man to thinke, that the historie of these daughters of Danaus is onelie of purpose deuised, and brought in place of Dioclesianus, to excuse the imperfection of our writers, whereas there was either no such historie (or at the least no such women that *Nennius.* arriued in this Ile) the authoritie of Nennius a Briton writer may be auouched, who wrote aboue 900. yeares past, and maketh mention of the arriuall of such ladies.

Belus priscus. *Danaidarium porticani. (text unclear)* To be short, the historie is thus. Belus the sonne of Epaphus, or (as some writers haue) of Neptune and

Libies (whome Isis after the death of Apis maried) had issue two sonnes: the first Danaus, called also Armeus; and Aegyptus called also Rameses: these two were kings among the Aegyptians, Danaus the elder of the two, hauing in his rule the Danaus. Aegyptus. *Higinus.* vpper region of Aegypt, had by sundrie wiues 50. daughters, with whome his brother Aegyptus, gaping for the dominion of the whole, did instantlie labour, that his sonnes being also 50. in number, might match. But Danaus hauing knowledge by some prophesie or oracle, that a sonne in law of his should be his death, refused so to bestow his daughters. Hereupon grew warre betwixt the brethren, in the end whereof, Danaus being the weaker, was inforced to flée his countrie, and so prepared a nauie, imbarked himselfe and his daughters, and with them passed ouer into Gréece, where he found meanes to dispossesse Gelenor (sonne to Stenelas king of Argos) of his rightfull inheritance, driuing him out of his countrie, and reigned in his place by the assistance of the Argiues that had conceiued an hatred towardes Gelenor, and a great liking towardes Danaus, who in verie deed did so farre excell the kings that had reigned there before him, that the Gréekes in remembrance of him were after called Danai.

But his brother Aegyptus, taking great disdaine for that he and his sonnes were in such sort despised of Danaus, sent his sonnes with a great armie to make warre against their vncle, giuing them in charge not to returne, till they had either slaine Danaus, or obtained his daughters in mariage. The yoong gentlemen according to their fathers commandement, being arriued in Greece, made such warre against Danaus, that in the end he was constrained to giue vnto those his 50. nephues his 50. daughters, to ioine with them in mariage, and so they were. But as the prouerbe saith, "In trust appeared treacherie." For on the first night of the mariage, Danaus deliuered to ech of his daughters a sword, charging them that when their husbands after their bankets and pastimes were once brought into a sound sléepe, ech of them should slea hir husband, menacing them with death vnlesse they fulfilled his commandement. They all therefore obeied the will of their father, Hypermnestra onely excepted, with whom preuailed more the loue of kinred and wedlocke, than the feare of hir fathers displeasure: for shee alone spared the life of hir husband Lynceus, waking him out of his sléepe, and warning him to depart and flée into Aegypt to his father. He therefore hauing all the wicked practises reuealed to him by his wife, followed hir aduice, and so escaped.

Pausanias. Now when Danaus perceiued how all his daughters had accomplished his commandement, sauing onelie Hypermnestra, he caused hir to be brought forth into iudgement, for disobeieng him in a matter wherein both the safetie and losse of his life rested: but she was acquitted by the Argiues, & discharged. Howbeit hir father kept hir in prison, and séeking to find out other husbands for his other daughters that had obeied his pleasure in sleaing their first husbands, long it was yer he could find any to match with them: for the heinous offense committed in the slaughter of their late husbands, was yet too fresh in memorie, and their bloud not wiped out of mind. Neuerthelesse, to bring his purpose the better to passe, he made proclamation, that his daughters should demand no ioinctures, and euerie suter should take his choise without respect to the age of the ladie, or abilitie of him that came to make his choise, but so as first come best serued, according to their owne phantasies and likings. Howbeit when this policie also failed, & would not serue his turne, he deuised a game of running, ordeining therewith, that whosoeuer got the best price should haue the first choise among all the sisters; and he that got the second, should choose next to the first; and so foorth, ech one after an other, according to the triall of their swiftnesse of foote.

How much this practise auailed, I know not: but certeine it is, diuers of them were bestowed, either by this or some other meanes, for we find that Autonomes was maried to Architeles, Chrysanta or (as Pausanias saith) Scea was matched with Archandrus, Amaome with Neptunus Equestris, on whome he begat Nauplius.

Higinus. But now to returne vnto Lynceus, whome his wife Hypermnestra preserued, as before ye haue heard. After he was once got out of the reach and danger of his father in law king Danaus, he gaue knowledge thereof to his wife, in *Pausanias.* raising a fire on heigth beaconwise, accordingly as she had requested him to doo at his departure from hir: and this was at a place which afterwards tooke name of him, and was called Lyncea. Upon his returne into Aegypt, he gaue his father to vnderstand the whole circumstance of the trecherous crueltie vsed by his vncle and his daughters in the murder of his brethren, and how hardly he himselfe had escaped death out of his vncles handes. Wherevpon at time conuenient he was furnished foorth with men and ships by his father, for the spéedie reuenge of that heinous, vnnaturall and most disloiall murder, in which enterprise he sped him foorth with such diligence, that in short time he found meanes to dispatch his vncle Danaus, set his wife Hypermnestra at libertie, and subdued the whole kingdome of the Argiues.

This done, he caused the daughters of Danaus (so many as remained within the limits of his dominion) to be sent for, whome he thought not worthie to liue, bicause of the cruell murther which they had committed on his brethren: but yet for that they were his wiues sisters, he would not put them to death, but commanded them to be thrust into a ship, without maister, mate or mariner, and so to be turned into the maine ocean sea, and to take and abide such fortune as should chance vnto them. These *Harding* and *Iohn Rouse* out of *David Pencair.* ladies thus imbarked and left to the mercy of the seas, by hap were brought to the coasts of this Ile then called Albion, where they tooke land, and in séeking to prouide themselues of victuals by pursute of wilde beasts, met with no other inhabitants, than the rude and sauage giants mentioned before, whome our historiens for their beastlie kind of life doo call diuells. With these monsters did these ladies (finding none other to satisfie the motions of their sensuall lust) ioine in the act of venerie, and ingendred a race of people in proportion nothing differing from their fathers that begat them, nor in conditions from their mothers that bare them.

But now peraduenture ye wil thinke that I haue forgotten my selfe, in rehearsing this historie of the ladies arriuall here, bicause I make no mention of Albina, which should be the eldest of the sisters, of whome this land should also take the name of Albion. To this we answer, that as the name of their father hath bene mistaken, so likewise hath the whole course of the historie in this behalfe. For though we shall admit that to be true which is rehearsed (in maner as before ye haue heard) of the arriuall here of those ladies; yet certeine it is that none of them bare the name of Albina, from whome this land might be called Albion. For further assurance whereof, if any man be desirous to know all their *Higinus.* The names of the daughters of Danaus. names, we haue thought good here to rehearse them as they be found in Higinus, Pausanias, and others. 1 Idea, 2 Philomela, 3 Scillo, 4 Phicomene, 5 Euippe, 6 Demoditas, 7 Hyale, 8 Trite, 9 Damone, 10 Hippothoe, 11 Mirmidone, 12 Euridice, 13 Chleo, 14 Vrania, 15 Cleopatra, 16 Phylea, 17 Hypareta, 18 Chrysothemis, 19 Heranta, 20 Armoaste, 21 Danaes, 22 Scea, 23 Glaucippe, 24 Demophile, 25 Autodice, 26 Polyxena, 27 Hecate, 28 Achamantis, 29 Arsalte, 30 Monuste, 31 Amimone, 32 Helice, 33 Amaome, 34 Polybe, 35 Helicte, 36 Electra, 37 Eubule, 38 Daphildice, 39 Hero, 40 Europomene, 41 Critomedia, 42 Pyrene, 43 Eupheno, 44 Themistagora, 45 Paleno, 46 Erato, 47 Autonomes, 48 Itea, 49 Chrysanta, 50 Hypermnestra. These were the names of those ladies the daughters of Danaus: howbeit, which they were that should arriue in this Ile, we can not say: but it sufficeth to vnderstand, that none of them hight Albina. So that, whether the historie of their landing here should be true or not, it is all one for the matter concerning the name of this Ile, which vndoubtedlie was See more in the description. called Albion, either of Albion the giant as before I haue said) or by some other occasion.

And thus much for the ladies, whose strange aduenture of their arriuall here, as it may séeme to manie & (with good cause) incredible, so without further auouching it for truth I leaue it to the consideration of the reader, to thinke thereof as reason shall moue him sith I sée not how either in this, or in other things of such antiquitie, we cannot haue sufficient warrant otherwise than by likelie coniectures. Which as in this historie of the ladies they are not most probable, yet haue we shewed the likeliest, that (as we thinke) may be déemed to agrée with those authors that haue written of their comming into this Ile.

But as for an assured proofe that this Ile was inhabited with people before the comming of Brute, I trust it may suffice which before is recited out of Annius de Viterbo, Theophilus, Gildas, and other, although much more might be said: as of the comming hither of Osiris, as well as in the Vlysses in Britaine. other parties of the world: and likewise of Vlysses his being here, who in performing some vow which he either then did make, or before had made, erected an altar in that part of Scotland which was ancientlie called *Iulius Solinus.* Calidonia, as Iulius Solinus Polyhistor in plaine words dooth record.

¶ Vpon these considerations I haue no doubt to deliuer vnto the reader, the opinion of those that thinke this land to haue bene inhabited before the arriuall here of Brute, trusting it may be taken in good part, sith we haue but shewed the coniectures of others, till time that some sufficient learned man shall take vpon him to decipher the doubts of all these matters. Neuerthelesse, I thinke good to aduertise the reader that these stories of Samothes, Magus, Sarron, Druis, and Bardus, doo relie onelie vpon the authoritie of Berosus, whom most diligent antiquaries doo reiect as a fabulous and counterfet author, and Vacerius hath laboured to prooue the same by a speciall treatise latelie published at Rome.

THE END OF THE FIRST BOOKE

9 789367 244616